WORDS FOR THE DEED

poems

Rodney Nelson

Published by Red Dashboard LLC
Publishing, Princeton NJ 08540
www.reddashboard.com

ACKNOWLEDGMENTS

Arts Pulse, The Beatnik, Big Bridge, Cape Journal, Connotation Press, Dead Drunk Dublin, Disquieting Muses Review, Elsewhere Journal, The Fence, Forty-Ounce Bachelors, The Green Door, Kerouac's Dog Magazine, Love Child Journal, Magic Cat Press, Stepping Stones Magazine, Vox Blaze, Words-Myth

CONTENTS

UNWINDING ROAD

for Britta Stein

the road that wound me away
to a deathtrap hotel in
                La Paz
                Baja
I had seen on the
                Rainy River
        and anywhere north
my foot that almost touched a
half-naked fan cord when I
was getting out of
                la ducha
       had
yet to arrive in
                Bangkok
      it seemed
will walk me toward living
                Chiricahua Peak
      any
time the road itself will unwind and
I may meet a trogon along it

SAN PEDRO

I have only driven the bridges
and a ways along it on the road north
not stopped and walked to let it win me
as any run of umbrage would in hard
desert
              I am in February
now and the cold and not of mountain mind
              even Chiricahua Peak and
              Glenn
                        fail to jibe in the imagination
the white rock height of which has drawn me
so during early May and early fall
              I have a
              trogon
                    a sora to
              meet and given a chance to pull off at
the cottonwoods I would render me
unto that land and river anytime

THUMP AND WAVER

the moment did not please
even if you were too young
to have acedia
the forenoon so bright gray that
it hurt your mind
                    you had
walked toward
                              Telegraph Hill
with a man you knew
                    the
woman you got it on with
was on a trip home to
                              Oregon
end of summer
not yet of the fog and
you could hear them getting set
to play
                              Quicksilver Mes-
                              enger Service
          at
                              Kearny
          and
                              Filbert
an outdoor
rally or demonstration
not what you had come to
                    what

you had come to who knew
and the music of the
moment did not draw
                not

                                rock
you might have come to hear
                some
                                Luciano Berio
were in this anyway
                the crowd
                the street
                the too-hard
                thump
                a waver of weed
you were a disappointed
child even if no one
had made you come or brought you
                helpless again
in the
hurt gray empty forenoon of
somebody else
                not the
man you knew who wanted to
shoot pool
                even if the
name of the
                                City
                had and
would have a chime to it
the year's would too
                                nineteen six-

                    ty five
              no that moment
only made acedia
into a carnival
you had to leave
              you were not
too young to have it then
              are
not too old now
              looking
              out on the monochrome
              prairie
                    March
              in a northern
              city
to like the thump
and waver of any day

SPRING

FROM THE SWEDISH OF BO BERGMAN

unkind spring is here now
with sun on roof and wall
your eyes run and your head is
emptier than a blown egg

you could even get sick
from all of this white light
glittering moving flashing
that's about to drown your house

glittering moving flashing
that hits it like a breaker
opening the innards
to public view and shock

VÅREN

Nu kommer den grymma våren
med sol i tak och vägg.
Mina ögon rinna, och hjärnan
är tom som ett urblåst ägg.

8

Man blir ju sjuk och fördärvad
av allt detta vita ljus,
som glittrar, glänser, vaggar
och dränker hela ens hus.

Det glittrar, glänser, vaggar
som långa böljeslag,
och rockens hål och själens
stå hemska i öppen dag.

WAIT

I cannot do anything but wait as I wait
cannot look at photos of a naked Mexico
in a magazine or write to anyone in
Manitowoc or toy with my radio until
I hear Luciano Berio
                    wait is to watch
and spring that has arrived in the light may not make it
to the ground unless I am on duty at the
window
                    watch is to wait
even in the night at night
most of all when so few are attuned to what might
come down anytime
                    wait is to wake
and I can move
then be a wakeman do it singing afoot to
note the hour and be listening to the chilly
dark until I hear a night bird's note of reply
                    wake is to wait
that spring may come to earth at watchcry

WORDS FOR THE DEED

to remember the whiff of the field is almost to have
one but mere agronomy of mind on a day
so late in March is not tenable
             tractor and drag are ready
will not await that crack in the cold much
longer and memories begin to madden
             edge up to
sense
             flaunt not only the odor of earth but its
good fallow hue where cultivation has exposed the clay
in it
             meadowlark reveille ahead of quick
darkening and thunder
             what early rain meant to the tongue
and what no one mind can have remembered
             the old
way to fallow
                          turn a furrow to the unplowed land and
                          returning turn over this furrow and the earth
                          on which the first one was laid
                          ribbling it close overthwart
and even the whiff of the words for the deed of
it on whatever morning
                          ribbling it close overthwart

RIVER UP

meeting of crow and man on railway bank
where levee joined it seemed more evitable than
flood even though neither one needed to
understand why water had risen
              crow picked at
wood flotage at edge of temporary
recession and man waited as though other had
had more right
              did not move or talk as crow
talked and hunted and stood for nothing and went up
away in April wind for nothing too

ON HOLY SATURDAY

flood going down on the other side of the
dike and what I might have said and was only
two feet deep around the willows now and the
aments in them were hanging waving a rich
yellow green in the south wind and higher lengths
of paven river walk were coming dry and
what I might have taken to be a mourning
cloak had lit too awkwardly on it that did
take off when I got there but kept returning
drunken-mothwise to my wine-red shirt and in
elder thicket were permanent nuthatch and
chickadee with a cranky new tone to them
and the side of the dike that had been under
was green already and though river did not
have much tumescence remaining having spilt
all of its rut in silt it went humping by
no matter what I might have said to wig it

NORTH DAM

I had made way through sun and odor
of plant rot to where I would have seen
the dam had flood gone down more and did
not want to get close to its moving
point of retreat which would have meant mud
              on the
other bank a muskrat went
with deliberation over a
dark wet stretch of siltage pausing now
to check on else that might be faring
which did not include me anymore
              had what
a musquash loved driven it
from what it loved and where and was it
back trying to find
              clean up
              redeem
or had the huge quick inundation
been only a game to it
              a side
of what it loved
              I thought but did not
whistle a rodent word to any-
thing or wait on an answer and knew
me as one of it as another

muskrat of lowth and lough-land prairie
with nowhere else to want to go or
be in the flood of my sporting time

START OF MAY

rain was making to come to start
another May and odor and
look of plum blossom walked me to
the river in latening day
that I crossed with half a notion
to avoid the known corner of
the lot ahead where someone might
have parked a car I would not
have known
                    half an eye detected
someone or two in motion and
I went north not using more of
it until I got to a tee
of street and avenue
                    waited
to look for traffic
                    pretended
to ignore what had not needed
to come to this intersection
that stopped and hared away in front
of me
                    a small car not daring
to be seen or to see that I
would not have known
                    though I did have
a whole notion that it lived south
and exiting the lot ought to

16

have turned and gone that direction
                    the one
it sped to take at the
next corner now
                    gone anyway
but someone stayed downtown in me
and walked me home before the rain

AT BUFFALOS' RIVER

I got there with a flit of cloud in
May noonlight and every shadow
brought a lowing on the prairie or
of it
               not of them or cattle and
I did not hear any lowing but
felt and saw the whole wide land react
when a cloud went through
            as if the dim
reminded it to moan the amount
of room there was to be alone in
            and
down the river were jays in
contention
             woods did not know moaning
now nor would I have thought to low where
I waited on a footbridge in the
sighed tenor of current
            wind among
            leaf
it had a soughing to it that
needed no me around
            that went back
to the time of them and earlier

OUR DAY

twinkle little Mozart music box
a Haydn finale is for tumbling class
public radio likes Telemann
and Boccherini even more and
on and on
                which period gives to
the baroque enlightened techie mind
around my everyday all it
has known to want but when I look out
of my window at a flowery
tree I hear another distant tune
                      I'll be with you in apple-blossom
                      time I'll be with you to change your name
                      to mine church bells will chime you will be
                      mine in apple-blossom time
              there is
phenology in the wind of a
northern May that has not yet hit hard
enough to deflorate it of a
white too meretricious anyway
on such a wimp tree
              a tune that had
                      antedated my prerococo
                      been revived to guide me on a trip
                      through orchards of Michigan forty-
                      one years ago in May

                    I have called
my sister at her botanica
out of town and
                              gotta be a crab
she thinks
                         would have to look at the leaf
and I talk to someone with the park
district
                                   oh ya that there's a spring-snow
                                   crabapple it don't bear any fruit
                                   the flower's sterile they like it as
                                   an ornament you know it had a
                                   parent tree the Siberian crab
maybe what I write is only an
ornament too and not the real pome
or poem from which verjuice and strong
green jack are made
                         any pip of which
can turn into a tree or the word
                    scrabapple
maybe cuckoo music
of baroque and rococo is all
that the spring-snow crab or I can write
                    if so
it is our day and the
techies of public radio need
not bother with Carl Ruggles even
at three in its morning
                         however
that may be I do not mind looking
out of my window in its now

who

would want to drive to a treacle tune
of nineteen twenty I'll be with you
in apple-blossom time through orchards
again not knowing amid scent and
color that what the heart at least had
chimed was sterile and ending with it

PRAIRIE FARMSTEAD

my living are gone for the day so I can
talk to my dead in the open here and walk
in the hard cool northwest wind as I might have
done with them
                        asparagus act manic and
a bobolink has to tack home to the doomed
alfalfa
                        they took and made of the farmstead
knew this midjune light and went
                        I could recite
tabulated name and date but only ask
them what will happen to it when my living
                        we living
follow
                        I want a guarantee
that no one lose it but cannot do any
hearing with all the roar in leaf and the dead
have quite a lag time too
                        I find their reply
in a Missouri cottonwood that has gone
high away over the box-elder slough
                        the
wooding my dead began that my living have
taken and made more of has grown off on an
own that no one can own
                        even if the land
were sold

the woods
cut
it would not be over
something would come up again
and something beat
into the hard June wind to a nest in it

IN THE WHILE

any glade in woods along the river and out
in older manmade woods would have come of fallage
on its own
                nettle not grass would have run in it
had there been not enough clearing
               the acremen
of the prairie had grown haven woods amid the
tillage
               leaving yard for an elm or two within
had created meadow also where a loner
tree that had not been cropped might have stood until it
got in the way
               the acrewomen with holly-
hock might have meant to draw an eye toward the house
               not so the
men with stook alee the grove
               a row
of which in early summer afternoon light might
have had beauty
               only they
would have seen it though
and basswood like them would have been at work into
the July flow of cottonwood seed
               it is that
               time now
and I have a tonnage of sweet yellow-
white to gawk up to

            an achieved unmoving mass
that only I can see
            man
            woman
            elm are dead
and their yard has become a glade with hollyhock
the meadow a weed claim with tree yet the achieved
time of basswood flower seems to want not to go
but to hang heavy and fragrant in the while now

RIVER DOWN

I am where they put an uglifying
clay-mud dike and took it away in the
flood month too but I had seen what pickings
for a crow on it
                   due green has prevailed
without due rain and an old friend of mine
                   the peach-leaf willow
is doing all right
next to the retreat of moving water
in July heat and only a mown part
has gone to dun
                   I am out of the sun
today where mosquitos belong and are
not and it may be time for a little
wind bathing
                   what would Seneca have thought

PRINCIPIUM/FINIS

hearty hard-hatted men are many with
          jackhammer
          backhoe
          forklift
          truck
and loud
in the downtown street
          it is the dawn of
all construction again and would revive
the pioneer in anyone
          this dog
day will get too hot but the sweatier
the work the holier
          I think of what
a man that Gore Vidal invented wrote
in a memoir

                  like most children of the
                  city I delight in its vitali-
                  ty and raw newness. The air is always
                  full of dust and the smell of mortar. The
                  streets are loud with hammering
          of some great
dorp on the hill in Alabama or
Kentucky you would imagine but the
town was
                  Constantinople
          back way when

what holied the work on it
            put Dothan
and Paducah in the light too and as
the guy in Vidal continued
                I find
                it a marvelous thing to be at the
                beginning of something great rather than
                at the end
            however
            the men in the
hot-lime vests and I are not where he was
are we or
                may I die today
            are we

TURN OR COME

not enough in the beginning of August
to write

                                the summer has turned

          or

                                come halfway
as though I were fixed to every morning
like an ordo on the wall

                had been waiting
with a note for incantation

                it may be
enough to write

                                a bobble in the heat

                and

                                more air than wind
to imagine me watching
the turn or come from the middle of the night
rain of it

                blowing along on what makes it

AUGUST TWELVE

it did not have to cloud or rain
in air like both that no wind moved
              only a suction
and I could
look into the grey-plum sky
              right
at a sun of intenser plum
and know a day had begun to
come that would not have to arrive
entirely
              would need to add
only its half or any part
to the grey unending stir of
wet and heat
              to yellow maybe

ON BROADWAY

sunlight had made it into the lounge of the gentrified
hotel and walking by windows I would not have put my
nose to I took quick note of men at a table
            were in
good business-casual the one proffering a buff-
and-orange literary magazine or annual
report and intimating how whatever he had read
in whichever had
                      absolutely electrified
            him
I imagined who already knew that the good life
and none other brought on good writing that men and women
of good taste had money that poetry like a coat of
arms did not come cheap but I had not needed to do the
lesson again
            I had known the hotel in its fleabag
heyday
            my dad when around had use to room there
            I knew
that Juan Ramón had been right and not Rainer Maria

CALIFORNIA HALL

no rain that winter night in a kind of wartime
and more than it could hold were there
    wanted to see
and hear the poets if they could
    mainly to be
at the reading and in a velveteen jumpsuit
Ferlinghetti strummed an autoharp and intoned
      get the hell outta
      here Doctor Hare
   McClure in
a leather jacket ran the word out to the crowd
in the street
    Levine did not have a blue collar
Brautigan did a navy p-coat and were smoke
and words and gallon jugs of wine but no mention
yet of the wanted hunted hero they meant to
raise money for
    the wife's late arrival brought that
word and from the lectern sumptuous Levertov
handed out syllabi that no one could pocket
    the very short
poem Brautigan read had the
name
     Rommel
    in it and a Bishop of too much
elegance and dignity got up also with
a cant on an earlier marked dark hero in

                    bedlam
and all had come to the hall this one time
in this time and city not only for a man
but to decry the kind of war going on in
the night around it and with smoke and wine and loud
poetry to celebrate the light they would make
within
                    so everyone belonged
                    elegant
                    other
it seemed everyone had moved toward
everyone
                    many would not belong again

JUAN RAMÓN TO RAINER MARIA

I knew the woman friend as well
that twitted you for snobbery
and how you tried to defend your
cultivation of princesses

their blood and jewelry you claimed
like a church wall or a castle
rampart were the olden time and
the olden tradition to you

you are lying at the foot of
a church wall of your own now in
Muzot and I am still here but
I have to ask you anyway

did you mean a benevolent
honest right tradition or the
tradition of mendacity
of indignity and cunning

the people of the countryside
are older and richer in the
true jewels of blood and song and
having lived out in the weather

are closer to rampart and wall
than your noble friends who twiddle

within and do not even know
the source of the protecting light

from *Aristocracia y democracia*,
prose text (1941); translation,
paraphrasis, and versification

AT THE MISSOURI

another family trip in childhood
might have done but one to the Mo happened
to do
        a look at the twin buttes at dawn
and I was not the world anymore
               men
had not yet flooded the cottonwoody
bottomland in which the river made me
distant
        it ran in the wild that I made
around me
            another T'ao Ch'ien
would well have done but Waley's would happen
to do
        I wanted to be that country

T'ao Ch'ien   Chinese poet (372–427 C.E.)
               "A heart that is distant creates
               a wilderness round it."
Waley's   Arthur Waley, translator

FARM MUSICKE

I did not imagine the song
> *clodhop with me to the steading*
> *where not only men may relax*
> *into cant*
      I heard it begin
in the field so long ago it
seemed like today
      only tried to
have imagined the singer
> *if*
> *a tree appose you root it out*
      came in toward the end I thought
a university twit as
metafarmkid he had to have
been and another of same sung
to
      or woman
but there was a
warm even freeboot tone to him
not room-learnt
> *and kick more than a*
> *gobbet off*
      mud no doubt

                    I could
imagine the ale the riant
mouth so long ago
                    only hear
the song begin in the plowing

ROCK DOVES ANYMORE

you were colombe and paloma in the rockery
a love unto one another when man found you so
and took you homing away but to come to the town
was down where dirtying a ledge or the head of a
casting of Colombo and your hemiolas in
air to a beat man did not get made you easy to
pigeonhole who were not even rock doves anymore
not even in the winter count and he may have plucked
an unfluttery word or two from you

PIGEONNEAU

PICHÓN

         but

listening under the concrete train bridge
he would find you a love unto one another so

NO WAITING

in a walkover the north wind had taken
the prairie and been maintaining cold on it
in an April without odor
                what matter
that daylight swole
                even out of the blow a
tree more waxwing than not had nothing for them
and not much bud so why were they to move
                    yet
the wind was hinting at a hint of mild now
which meant that a shift had come to Flin Flon too
the start of a changeover
                I would have had
to wait to watch the ironwood tree of the
desert flower and here was a waxwing tree

FIFTEEN APRIL

spring came late and quiet for everyone
on the prairie but in a way not for you
old man though you are in a late quiet time
where you sun and wind-bathe next to the river
and a mudded log that the flood put here on
what are now the rudiments of green
             had the
spring meant you to trill and nest and breed it would
have come for you but it may have intended
you for compost only the notion of which
need not quirk an old man's meditativeness
             you have
no children to feud with so do not
wear an abrahamic beard and no one at
home to remind you to take a cane when you
go out
             no home
        you do not have to have a
cane are good to run but know after many
an April that there is no one nothing to
run to or from
        it is three o'clock and warm
in the north the wind having spent and you have
not moved old man may not even see the box-
elder bug in front of your own open eye

BASTWOOD

on twenty-six April I went to a town park
but seemed to be in the woods of it already
not late in the month or any time even though
beginning leaves told of one
             to be not only
at the tree I wanted to walk around and the
other trees that meant as much where I had yet to
arrive
             seemed to be near a woods of memory
as well to which I had run from childhood and I
could see it high and thick in the oxbow it filled
hear a chitter that belonged to the park morning
I came to now
             maybe to all the woods I had
known in a picture that each only added to
in the way that
                      ett lass
                      ett gammalt hjulspår
            I
            had found under ragweed in
                   maderna kring ån
where immigrants had dropped the language too
                 had turned
into part of it and I seemed to be walking
around the tree I had wanted to walk around
and at the same or any or no time at all
arriving where the tree I had begun to see

from
                    maderna kring ån
          on another or same
morning awaited no eye of mine to be here

                    ett lass   a wagon
                    ett gammalt hjulspår   an old cart rut
                    maderna kring ån   the sloughs around the river

                    from *Aftonland* by Pär Lagerkvist
                    copyright © 1953 by Albert Bonniers Förlag

43

GOOD HOPE

every one in seven years I make land in Table
Bay and know that I am meeting Dora again who will
haven me in her hold this time, not damn and turn me back
to the deck of my command, my never rounding of the
cape, I can tell how long ago it was that I did worse
than flout her, I killed the love we had, denied it then, to
writhe and clinch with a young fishwife, because today will mark
my seventh return to squinch in the daylight of the town
until I hear Dora's greeting, we thought you were dead, and
move toward it, until I wake at the cottage to the
same valediction, we'll see you in a week, watch her put
on a shawl and leave, forty-nine years, will be a seventh
waiting to commit once more to the dinghy, to assault
on a cape of which I descry the gleamy headland but
that is only storm and midnight when I approach, surfeit
of port and other woman let me not wait the first week,
made me want away, so I put out in the evening
to round the cape and a wind that no one had foretold of
set me onto the rocks, I had ship remaining to try
again, over and ever, every one in seven
years a remit it seemed, making land and hearing Dora,
we thought you were dead we know you went down, telling the
    one
I loved to pardon and take me in now so that I would
not have to go back to my damned command, in the night a
promise, in the valediction none at all, maybe I
did go down I have thought as I row or am rowed to

anchorage, the mirror has nothing in it, of my crew
I would recognize not any a man jack if I saw
him, Dora is unchanged, a wealth of dark-gold hair in wind
when I am landward and she is coming to the jetty
that I want to reach, hear the call again even though I
have to redivine the meaning in it, the town has not
changed either, should have by now the seventh septennary,
and why has nobody joined her, everyone has to have marked
me lying off, putting to, not a death ship yet, but the
walks are vacant in the din of light, I was drunk when I
weighed anchor that first evening and if I spat at the
devil would not know, we'll see you in a week, it might have
been her own curse of the moment on me she withdrew in
worser pain when I went down which left me tided to the
cape even so but with a chance every seventh year
to make land in Table Bay, today the morning of the
seventh seventh year I am in the dinghy, my glass on
the path she will take to meet whatever I am, but I
am not rowed or rowing on, you have forgiven whom most
can't be my love the wind that I went into was meant to
right the account you should have let me drown with the rest oh
we'll not see you in even a week, I try to call this
to my Dora, the week has ended and maybe I can

       heave a last anchor up and put
       about, the headland astern, make
       seaway toward the haven of
       all dead men and true in the west

UNTIL RAIN

river not quite diluvian ran full
and quick in much-awaited warm that let
it have scent now
                opened memories in
                        a man
                the way for a pinch of green on
                the black mud and a plat of it higher

earth to him and wet gray leaf amounted
to a farm or two he had known and the
idea of a willowed other that
he knew of but
                        I am an animal
                he had to say
                        I
                        a man animal
                        remember only
                        what I need to keep
                        moving

he would not have to bename the
ghost women of that willowed height or moan
each within her time
                they were all upstream
on it and thunder would wake out the rest

of the green
                              it
                  had budded today
                  he
needed to remember only this white-
throated sparrow to move on
until rain

WINDOW

eve of May on streetlit pavement
and dead leaf on move again in
wind moment
    cellophane wrapper
turning with it around around
having to wait with it now and
no color to new leaf of tree
in half-night
    no name I used to
know to anything and I will
be turning again tomorrow

VISIBILITY OF THE FAMILIAR

wet-wind sky added to gravity
but dandelion in meadow next
to river meant up
                not only grass
would own its color now with leafing
way out in willow some too airy
for touch in oak
                prairie would withdraw
and town be woods have honeysuckle
in flower
                where swaling got down to
mud though a totally green elder
that flood had worked at leant into gray
river not meaning it but hermit
thrush were several at the feet of
what many stood
                        chipping sparrow few
              higher in
town were spring-snow crab to
make daylight a muted sky would not
and the familiar visible

OTHER IDES

river had gone rampant on time
but with more inflow than its width
could take would not subdue and went
swollen like a man to marry
again into the ides of May
           the Red
for all that weight was not
too old to cut a meander
and make a meadow of risen
carp in the bottomland not now
with the Otter Tail feeding it

COMING BACK

swift fox had known time ago
the prairie I would meet who
had not heard of them or them
were killed out before and I
had not even read the name
until a report of three
run over one downvalley
a few miles
                    they were coming
back to a death at the road
without inherited or
learnt foxery to avoid
the man machine in country
they would have to run to know
once more but more arriving
would effect this and if I
outlive me I may hear the
young of them moving in a
ring on a moon night talking
of met prairie that I shall
have met and known time ago

EARLY CHILDHOOD WITH ANNELIDA

wind had sung without word in the silo
but in morning came the still and wet and
cloud only thin to a mere horizon
of tent and truck at mud field's other edge
        words carrying on now
        through damp
            not known
and no matter how bright the forenoon grayed
were carp and garter snake and bullhead in
muck enough to match were snapping turtle
in brick tank was a hut that earthworm lent
to man and skunk
        at beginning of heat
        time and the slime
other words carrying
and now an immediate known man's
           you
           hear dem people talking
           can you
           vell ven
           you grow up you yist
           better watch out for
           dem Mexicali Roses
of which the
hearer would hear no more until came a

song at manhood swell with word to draw him
back happy and humble to the miring
Annelida of origination

TIME IN A STATE PARK

for Britta Stein

wet woods a corroboree
of mosquito infringing

but on the open I had
an escort of dragonfly

with some drift web and other
touching my arm now or when

had I been wearing a watch
I might not have lived to this

FLOODING INTO JUNE

innings of only water over the diamond
in light of the loon and at noon an unending train
of flotsam wood in midcurrent
              if a man went up
on a bridge to watch it the river might get him that
will make the swallows out of home in a half hour
and he would have no height to turn to or thrown line to
grab at this off time
              no one around the rising
                    all
off to dike and ward it and not many crows and an
eagle and he are here to hunt or scavenge only

SORTIE AT BUFFALO RIVER

that day even week seemed not to be in June
with air more than cool and the light uncertain
but wood tick were hunting in oak and tallgrass
and tent caterpillar had done the meant work
           that day
might have been in June but only on
the tundra when the air went heavy and a
wind took the rain and toed it into shelter
even swan time might have come again to the
not-meant place
               you would have heard a trumpeting
not seen the all-ready pink of a June rose

LOST IN THE MORAINE

was early or not for cottonwood to seed
never to be out walking on the high till
whether to the grassy top of a drumlin
or among the lower onetime braided streams
that oak grew on and had been as erratic
as we were now on the way to a kettle

a dip with water in it a fen kettle
anyway of no draw to us while the seed
of cottonwood moved around the erratic
where we rested and we did not go on till
some definite tending in the braided streams
seemed to manage us toward the right drumlin

which turned out to be just another drumlin
and from the top of it we saw a kettle
maybe the very one that the braided streams
had taken us to with the cottonwood seed
maybe another we could not tell in till
where perception moments became erratic

yet that would have had to be the erratic
we had rested at en route to this drumlin
right or not we figured but knew that the till

had many of such by many a kettle
which put enough doubt in our mind to seed
a lot of cottonwood in the braided streams

a braiding of perception created streams
that did not lead anywhere an erratic
tending to the downdrift of cottonwood seed
we would have to follow to any drumlin
hoping we would reach at another kettle
our starting point in the end of the till

it was not too late to be out walking till
dim went down into the onetime braided streams
took away the very notion of kettle
at which our footing became erratic
and we did not look up at the right drumlin
when we got to it with the cottonwood seed

we would not have a kettle or a drumlin
in any sure view till the cottonwood seed-
ed the erratic braiding or our mind streams

SHOW AND SHADOW

in an old gray movie a warplane went up the runway
into a sky of no color that seemed to ache with the
music and the woman's look who had waved to it and him
and all remaining of the military plane and man
was a driblet of exhaust on cloud and watching him off
hurt because the two had not gotten to the needed words
or omitted them might not have a chance to meet again
and rain was coming she might want to die yet the rain that
other men had written was real so too runway and sky
in the madeup narrative tingeing them
        I do not know
how late in life I am cannot remember the ending
of what I saw in a crummy show hall of childhood but
this afternoon when a navy exhibition team bucked
the hot damp air I knew the narrative had not changed or
ended even if these warplanes were not of no color
              I
wonder if I turned into that departing man he
into me and went away into more than sky I mean
time if the woman knew me when I got back if she had
waited had we said the needed words or did I fly too
early am I beyond the aching and the music now

ENVOI

what I remember seeing was a picture of rain not
rain and an arranged interpretation of worry on

59

a white face that had not belonged to the woman in the
narrative who whatever might have happened would not have
survived the forgotten ending
                    I had smelt the movie
theater not the aviation fuel or any
perfume but the invented emotion had made it hard
for the man on duty and me to leave and it has clung

NINETEEN-OH-SEVEN

rain had made too thick a river lode in
May to June for the given outtake and
its slime water had to come up then it
receded only enough to let the
matted gray of drowned plant be seen and smell
iodinic in the heat but the men
of my mind their wheat sown rode stoneboat on
the prairie taking huge drift rock to heave
in a tree claim and the I of my mind
drove the team in Swedish until what had
to have been a late June afternoon went
not so glary white to the eye and the
men and I of my mind walked in ease to
the river knowing the hard good work to
be done and the evening words ahead
and I could have imagined them today
on my very way to that matted bank
with everyone gone and me alone
me a moving unintended scarecrow

OLD MAN SUMMER

had no form or children
did have a breath and yards
of ragweed and maybe
a widow Rena to
whom were left headache
and heat
            a back way to her
hut in the nodding town
went through willow and wild
asparagus so few
beyond flicker knew it
and the porch way remained
too quiet in a noon
that did not end
            old man
summer had no form or
children
            would have an end
be widowing Rena
again in golden rod

TWENTY-SEVEN JULY

I was taking a path that went into country
to lake and thicket and gravel pit I knew but
on this dog midday of a waxing month I did
not let kingbird into mind and would have only
as another word in a fourth goodbye
                         event
or nonevent seemed to ready and need it now
even if mailing would have made it a last and
I kept at the word in the shadow of me on
a track that went into light to weed jumble and
snag I had known when writing and cormorant and
May were like one
                  but night would have a fulling moon
I might have sensed too or it might have been no more
than common hunch telling me I had made up my
own nonevent to go back go back right away
that let the kingbird into mind and tree again

AFIELD

campus within greater north campania in the heat
and direct lighting of July and poeta doctus
not around to fondle his vivarium with an eye
the vine-propp elme the builder oake and the laurel meed of
mightie conquerours but would return anon to hold the
trimmed environment once more the only vegetation
he knew would nod in mortarboard and gown for how but in
custom and ceremony did one reverence the day
let a poem be of it littera scripta manet
maybe have a field night with the gesta romanorum
and I did not see him now even a nymph among
the goodly flowres wherewith dame nature doth her beautifie
had never looked to poeta doctus anyway and
with a chance to go into his field I walked right through
went afield on the unmown greater north campania

campania   (L.) open field
poeta doctus   (L.) learned poet
the vine-propp elme, et seq.   from *The Faerie Queen*, Edmund Spenser
for how but in, et seq.   from "A Prayer for My Daughter," William Butler
    Yeats
littera, et seq.   (L.) the written letter keeps
the goodly, et seq.   Spenser, op. cit.

HARBOR NIGHT

there had been saxophone on radio in
the apartment we drove away from toward
a known-or-not hill in a city that turned
rain port by day would not harbor lights or get
warm until that brown-purple evening when
we saw a row of them it had to do with
the hill we were coming to so knew or not
and we were old and very young
                           ahead would
be taillights in the road toward a dirt port
the memory of later music but the
night into which a hued evening had changed
would not change we were not very young and old
might have seen everything in that row of
lights on a known-or-not hill we were coming
to would be coming to or are we passing

WALKER'S INTERIM

hawk had looked at walker so made
him turn in time to see it leave
the branch and dip toward one east
of the river that had nothing
human around it
                              light again
                    would have been a farm and harvest
there the heavy itchy clothes in
damp heat of binding or swathing
a yelled name that walker might have
read in an album and hawk known
and now were not
                              only weed field
                    urban thrum
at the edge and section number
would not mean much to the next to
come nor had to in a walker's
interim pioneering when
even hawk was arbitrary

ANYHOW

month of an end to come but nothing
outright melancholic in virid
late high summer
                heat easing
                            not much
wind or urgency around the dry
grove and ragweed up now not fading

wren time done but the education
of many other fledging to start
yet no hurry about it or to
the contenting daylight's underplay
                            I am
                worried anyhow as if
a one-only god were mad at me
for not having thought or done what the
midsummer of his making wanted

LAKE OF THE WOODS

I had to come to this much water
to this hard true beach and shell and wood
not wanting to read
                    having written
my would and shall I wanted this wind
to happen on me where I might not
have been as it did on the lake now
I had to hear in my sleep the hum
of big water continuing a
jack-pined half mile away as if I
were not anyone there but a shell
or wood fragment of all that was
                              I
wanted to read that beach
                    would and shall

HARVEST HOME

memory had taken and kept their motion and big
machines out on a cut field and I was in a grove
lane watching would have been made to know the men
had to do with me and were right and good and the heat
was only another's word to a too-young child but
at twenty I sweat knew every word if threshing
machine and steam engine were gone with Granduncle Ernst
and I had not worn denim overall a straw hat
of so wide a brim that in noonlight no one could make
out the wearer I did not attach good or right to
the onetime field tableau how long a belt joined machine
to racketing engine in a whirl of chaff the tree-
dark on either side of the lane framing it nor would
I even visit the grove now Granduncle Albin's
domain who did not welcome a young-man relative
the memory getting distanter but the took and
kept returns to me in age and I can see them move
to the threshing of light or the wheat it became and
the work a dance not drudgery I hear them belling
trave tröska over the racket a triumph note
of the moment on land where light used to be grama
and fire the reaping and I have to go in my
dirty gester boots with the men to the dim hot yard
intoning their harvest home as only right and good

> trave   sheaf pile
> tröska   thresh

HOLIDAY WEEKEND IN TOWN

I was not out in the afternoon
but ovened in its quiet
   I walked
waited on a meadow May flooding
had mudded that lay cracked and patchy-
green and the river trees had wealth in
that color but vacation among
them
     not much movement to watch
     or sound
        maybe a thin
        infrequent chirr
        a
        fading red squirrel
        maybe cricket
some old man and woman I had known
who knew me might have looked out with a
tired wave but I could not have seen them
and did not want anyone to be
       there
    in the grove
I was in time not
quite spent and went to round and touch
a friend the giant peach-leaf willow
at where high water had come and would
again
     every drooping thing out

              of it
                        every
                        mushroom
                        on it
              were
active unfaded in the damp
hot shade of the summer day to which
a cottonwood added one gold leaf

DAWN RAIN

heat and major daylight had made it
to evening ahead of the clouds
but half dark at seven again did
not grant morning only a rain
umbration
           walk and rooftop black wet
                a day
                sick with weather
        I might have
        written or
                weeping
                claustrophobic
                dying of shadow
                not enough air
my windowpane not at all warm
        yet
I knew apnea and illness were
a worry of word this side of it
lachrymosity and cloistration too
that out in gray light another rock
dove would mount to a ledge forever

ON ROSH HASHANAH

migrant flicker and jay were here
not home but had a part in the
nonhuman town activity
that fleeted around the human
was hard to track until a leaf
wagged in tree or hedge
              not much home-
bird movement to it
                    flicker and
jay were not home here but were
                  as
           on the known airway
           to the Gulf
the unafraid white heron too
hunting a pond that men had made
in July and getting no catch
and out of town at a remote
pothole a phalarope trio
waited on what was all their own
more home here even if they found
the mud side of it only twice
a year
              keeping to it no more
than other migrants did to town

TOWARD AUTUMN

monarch rallying in a butterflies' week
to hurry away together maybe flee
what would come
           jigging in no one direction
now among heavy grass and ragweed in flower
to end with dragonflies' time a turning of
sumac by the hill and again an orange
dot
           the monarch penultima
           readying
to leave and whichever insect to drop an
egg the nodding grass to lay seed on the wind
until the fade at sundown but how many
uncommon merganser working anyway
           a low dark flight of them
           hurrying quiet
over the lake to be ahead of what would
come yet no one direction now or ever
to the dragonflying nor urgency
                no
           need to leave
           only moving
           to stay maybe
in the huge red granite somehow hoven out
of the gentle bottomland havening cacti
with aster come what might
           butterfly and duck

not fleeing either not hurrying just
drawn away by what would draw egg and seed in

EVEN-NIGHT DAY

osprey outmaneuvering wind high
in returned heat I tolerated
among white heath-aster bloom
                        the too-
                        red sumac
            wanting to chew the seed
of it
                        take onto me
            burnishment
not tarnishing of green in the few
cottonwood
                        hunt
            the unlimited
open around that man had named a
sparrow for but the pothole water
would not all heat without much fund of
sun
                        even even-night midday marked
a move to deplete
                        a clammying

ABOUT THE AUTHOR

Rodney Nelson's home region, the Red River prairie, has been called a valley but is in fact a seabed with hidden beaches rimming it. To the west are the Missouri coteaux and higher plains and the Badlands. Nelson likes to wander in the region, always on the lookout for poems.

He began as a poet quite a few years ago but turned to fiction in midcourse, not returning to poetry until the 2000s. A lifelong nonacademic, he has worked in California as a licensed psychiatric technician and Arizona as a copy editor. Nelson's other poetry books include *Metacowboy, In Wait, Mogollon Picnic, Bog Light, Sighting the Flood,* and *Fargo.* He lives in the latter North Dakota city.

www.reddashboard.com

JUN 0 1 2015

9 781503 115781